THE BIRMINGHAM CANAL NAVIGATIONS
THROUGH TIME
R. H. Davies

AMBERLEY PUBLISHING

Acknowledgements

This publication would have been impossible without the kind and generous assistance of those who allowed me to use their wonderful photographs. This includes Geoff Walton (GW); Keith Hodgkins (KH), Tipton historian who has such an extensive collection; David Wilson (DW), who also took many canal photos just as the carrying days were coming to a close; Dr T. Daniels (DTD), who has written so much about Oldbury and Langley; Ruth Collins, for images from the extensive William King collection (WK).

First published 2010

Amberley Publishing Plc
Cirencester Road, Chalford,
Stroud, Gloucestershire, GL6 8PE

www.amberley-books.com

Copyright © R. H. Davies, 2010

The right of R. H. Davies to be identified as the Author of this work has been asserted in accordance with the Copyrights, Designs and Patents Act 1988.

ISBN 978 1 4456 0225 7

British Library Cataloguing in Publication Data.
A catalogue record for this book is available from the British Library.

Typeset in 9.5pt on 12pt Celeste.
Typesetting by Amberley Publishing.
Printed in the UK.

Introduction

Tick tock goes the clock, time marches on, and the world – our world changes. Usually it's a gradual process and you hardly notice the difference; sometimes it's more dramatic, especially if you move back to an area you have known intimately. Yes, we humans are ever aware of that influential fourth dimension, whether consciously or unconsciously. And the purpose of this book is to use photographs to compare some of those changes to the landscape and, to be specific, to the Birmingham Canal Navigations, or the BCN.

The Birmingham canals truly got underway following an advertisement in Birmingham's *Aris's Gazette* of 26 January 1767. The plan was simple, though the organisation and construction did have its own peculiar complications. It was to take a narrow waterway from Wolverhampton through the growing towns of Bilston, Tipton, Oldbury and Smethwick, through to the heart of industrial Birmingham, with an additional branch to Lord Dudley's coal mines on the hill overlooking Wednesbury. The five-mile branch to Wednesbury via the first junction at Spon Lane, West Bromwich, was completed first in 1769; four years later and the canal was connected to the Staffordshire & Worcestershire Canal at Aldersley just outside Wolverhampton. The S&W thus connected the first Birmingham canal to the outer world. From that date on, the network grew in leaps and bounds, with many more branches and connections right through to the 1860s. The final great additions were the Tame Valley Canal, the Netherton Tunnel of 1858, and then a little later the Cannock Extension Canal and Church Bridge locks and branch, making a further connection to the S&W.

And now, anyone remotely interested in the Black Country canals will trot out the familiar statistics that, by that time, the BCN had over 160 miles of canal, including 206

❀❀❀❀❀❀❀❀❀❀❀❀❀❀❀❀❀❀❀❀❀❀❀❀❀❀❀❀❀❀
BIRMINGHAM, Jan. 24, 1767.

THE Utility of a Navigable Cut from the Wolver-hampton Canal, 'through the Coal Works, to this Town, having been pointed out in a preceding Paper, by which (exclufive of the other Emoluments) it appears that the Town will reap a confiderable Advantage in the Maintenance of its Poor, a Meeting, for the further Confideration of this Scheme is thought effentially neceffary ; therefore the Conftables, Churchwardens, and Overfeers, do hereby give public Notice, That a Meeting will be held on Wednefday next, at Six o'Clock in the Afternoon, at the Swan Inn in this Town, at which the Gentlemen and Inhabitants are fo-licited to attend, in order (if the Scheme fhall be approv'd) that a proper Perfon be appointed to Survey and give an Eftimate of the Canal in Queftion, and that fuch other Propofals may be offered as may feem moft likely to an-fwer the intended Purpofe.

Advertisement in *Aris's Gazette* for the new Birmingham canal.

locks, seventeen pumping station, seven tunnels, six reservoirs of that most precious commodity, water, and literally dozens of junctions and links with other canals and railways. As for the landscape, certainly when the navvies dug the initial Brindley Canal, they worked their way through mainly open heath and farm land, and there are definitely no images from this era, but you can get a rough idea of what the area was like if you take a visit to Sutton park. From the beginning, coal mines and ironworks flourished until, by the beginning of the twentieth century, every kind of industry filled the space between Birmingham and Wolverhampton.

Many of the photographs in this book portray that smoke-filled landscape, with its brick-built factories and back-to-back housing. Coal was always the largest commodity carried on the BCN, and it fed a coal-based economy, with iron a close second. Nevertheless, the demand for coal dropped sharply after the Second World War, and it appeared to some folk during the 1950s and 1960s that the BCN would be gradually lost to the land developer. And here is the second well-known fact, that during that period of change, the BCN did lose sixty of its miles; most were unceremoniously filled in and built over. Nevertheless, canal enthusiasts, coupled with a slowly growing leisure trade started to make an appearance. Alongside this movement, many of the Midlands manufactories steadily moved from heavy to lighter and higher technological industries. Also, towards the end of the twentieth century, people desired a more attractive, clean and green environment.

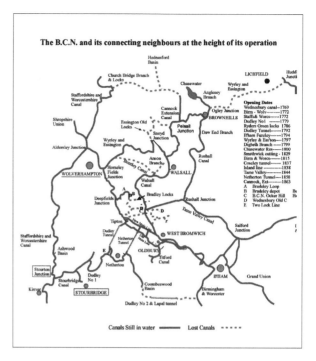

Map of the Birmingham canals showing the connections to its neighbours. Lost canals have been depicted with a dotted line.

Coal miners fixing a roof support timber at Homer Hill pit. (CM)

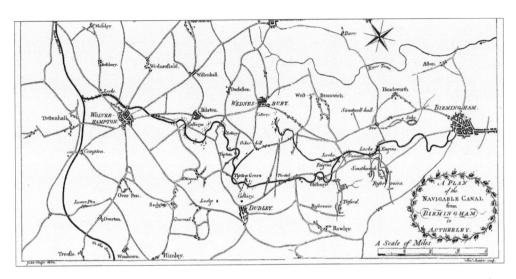

One of the early plans for a navigable canal from Birmingham to Autherley and its rather convoluted course via Smethwick, Oldbury, Tipton and Bilston. (The junction is now called Aldersley – Autherley Junction is about half a mile away.)

Archaeological dig of 2010 where the Baskerville basins used to lie. This area will be the foundation for the new Birmingham library.

Baskerville House to the right, and Millennium Place in front in 2010. The new library will be just beyond Baskerville House.

5

Birmingham

Birmingham seemed to lead the way in redevelopment, while others such as Wolverhampton and Walsall have been slow to utilise the natural attractions of a waterfront setting. Even the old industrial towns of Tipton, Wednesbury and Oldbury started to build modern housing around their canals in the latter part of the twentieth century, though maybe without the grandiose architectural designs of their larger neighbour. Within these pages, I have tried to comprehensively cover the major areas of the BCN, namely Birmingham, Smethwick, Oldbury, West Bromwich, the Dudley and Stourbridge canal system, Wolverhampton, and last but not least, Walsall and Pelsall. You always miss something out and I can only apologise, but in the end the wealth of photographs, or indeed dearth of such dictates the collection to a great extent.

Of course, development never stops, and recently Birmingham Council has decided to build a new library, not far from the old one. In the process of digging the foundations, the remains of some of the oldest of the city's canals were unearthed. A news item stated,

> During July and August 2009, Birmingham Archaeology were involved in a lucrative project in the centre of Birmingham. Excavations have exposed the site of an extensive brass working complex of the type that the city was famous for during the nineteenth century. The manufactory made decorative brass objects such as bedsteads and house fittings. The site began to be developed on the 1820s following the cutting of the canal arm around 1811. A large brass rolling and wire drawing mill was constructed along the north side of the canal. The whole site was extended to include workshops and furnaces.

And so, Birmingham's industries started to expand, all promoted by the arrival of the canal, and you can see where that initial expansion was if you turn to the Birmingham map and see where it shows Baskerville wharves. Mr John Baskerville incidentally was a Birmingham eccentric who had made a fortune from the printing industry just prior to the arrival of the canal. His house and garden were amongst the first things to go as the canal expanded.

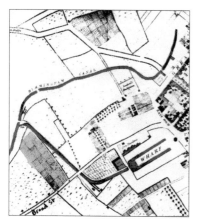

Hanson's survey map of 1778 shortly after the introduction of the canal (1772) depicts two termini of the Birmingham–Wolverhampton canal. The southern terminus ends in a forked wharf, opposite Paradise Street, where eventually the BCN offices came to be. The northern terminus ended at Friday Bridge, just beyond Crosby's Wharf. Notice that the land around the canal and its junction is rural; in fact, the map shows meadows and garden-style allotments where Brindley Place will eventually come to be. The first sign of industry around the canal is the iron foundry next to the forked (old) wharf.

The second stage of the canal's development is shown on this map, where Telford's canal alterations and improvements of the late 1820s have formed a loop on the old canal. But notice the growth of activity that has taken place through the ensuing fifty years. Gas Street Basin has been born, with its own gas company to power the lighting system. The Old Wharf is being used by the Birmingham Coal Co., and the BCN offices are in place. A brass works now stands on Brindley Place. A second coal wharf is on the loop owned by Rollansons, and more coal wharves come off Gas Street. Birmingham is no longer a canal cul-de-sac but a vibrant hub of inland waterway operations, with the Newhall Branch, and the Birmingham–Worcester Canal well established and going out of the city north and south respectively. Coal was the great commodity brought into the town, and a poet of the time, John Freeth, wrote a song of the canal:

> Then revel in gladness let harmony flow
> From the district of Bordesley to Paradise Row
> For True feeling joy in each breast must be wrought
> When coals under five pence per hundred are brought.

Oddly enough, Baskerville had been buried, according to his will, upside down in his own garden, and as the navvies arrived he had to be dug up again. Today, Baskerville House stands as a memorial to this Birmingham worthy, and at the front of the building stands a group of oversized printing blocks with the typeface that he designed.

Our first map depicts Birmingham a short while after the canal arrived in 1769. The canal has a junction which we now call Old Turn, and the northern arm terminated a hundred yards or so away, while the other branch terminates at a twin wharfing area where the company later built its major offices. Gas Street Basin developed right at the bend near the wharfs – while they disappeared along with the company offices in the early twentieth century. Only an ornamental bridge now hints at their previous existence.

Our second map, from around 1830, shows the development of Gas Street Basin and the gasworks is in red. Birmingham's early show hall – Bingley Hall – is also right next to the canal and has been replaced by the far more glitzy and glamorous Convention Centre. Opposite Gas Street Basin lie more coal wharves, along with stone and timber wharves and brick kilns. Interestingly, our modern Brindley Place was then still occupied by small gardens!

What News Items Said About Birmingham's Modern Development

The old hidden world of Birmingham's canals of the nineteenth and early twentieth centuries have, since the 1970s, received a complete transformation of image, impressing visitors and locals alike. A courageous city council, along with highly skilled architects, and the developers Argent, have created a bright, new, mixed-use urban neighbourhood. And it is fervently hoped that this careful balance of leisure, retail, business and residential property will provide an enjoyable and sustainable environment. London has had its own flagship development schemes, but Brindley Place provides valuable lessons for other cities and towns, with water frontage, wishing to emulate its grand success.

Maybe some of you who have slightly longer memories, and lived near to Birmingham, recall a centre stifled by an inner ring road, loads of ghastly concrete, and a sad decayed canal environment, set in high canyons of disused and gloomy brickwork. Much of that has now gone – and we can all benefit from a vision that has created attractive spacious pedestrian areas, set on a variety of levels, with sculptures and other eye-pleasing architectural features and buildings. But there is no doubt that a vision was required for that transformation, and much credit goes to Birmingham city council for assisting in that highly imaginative strategy for Brindley Place, and the canal centre. The earliest master plan for the area was drawn up by Terry Farrell, with assistance on pedestrian flows from Bill Hillier, and later the plan was revised by John Chatwin in collaboration with the main developer Argent, who secured the site for a comparatively small £3 million following a property crash. From then on, good working relationships between the council, architects and contractors brought about the superb development that we have today.

Birmingham's Brass House

In the late eighteenth century, brass workers in Birmingham relied on prices set by brass houses in other parts of the country. It was decided that a local centre was needed to try and stabilise price fluctuations. Two hundred proprietors came together, each raising £100 to set up the centre, and as a result, the brass house was established in 1781, and the price of brass went from £84 to £56 per ton. Brass and brass articles were to be made from this site next to the canal until 1850. The furnaces and chimneys were demolished in 1906, and the Birmingham Water Co. took over the main building. In the early 1800s, pins from brass wire were one of many items being made, and by 1824, a machine had been designed that could turn out 150 per minute. These pins were sold by drapers and haberdashery shops.

In 1860, a Mr Stephen Jarrett, a pin maker from Gloucester, came to Birmingham and joined forces with Mr Charles Rainsford, and they had a factory on Broad Street. In November 1860, their employees earned around £1 2s 6d per week, working a ten-hour day six days a week. By 1880, their wages had increased to about £3 6s per week. However, Birmingham made many articles from brass in this area. James Collins made fittings for cabinets, and ship and railway fittings. The Atlantic Clock Works existed from 1865, and Morris's Art Metal Works manufactured hearth implements and beauty boxes. Among many others on the former Brindley Place site was the Washington Works, making steel pins up to 1910, Mr Parker an ironmonger, and the engine works belonging to G. E. Bellis, who made steam compressors.

The largest building on Oozels Street was the red brick, four-storey Atlas Works. This sat on the site that has now become the Sea Life Centre. From 1887 to 1958, it was the premises of T. E. Wales & Son, and they manufactured wire mattresses and beds and were the largest bedding manufacturers in the Midlands.

Developers were invited by the city council to draw up a blueprint for an area of 26 acres next to the International Convention Centre (across the canal from Brindley Place) in July 1987, and the site was leased to a consortium of three companies – Merlin, Shearwater and Laing (MSL). They planned a huge leisure and entertainment area after their experience in Baltimore, USA. They paid £23 million for the development rights, and went on to construct the National Indoor Arena. A National Aquarium and a monorail system linking to the city were all in the original plans.

The *Evening Mail* reported that a £28 million deal had been struck, to convert rundown Broad Street into the international showpiece of Birmingham after months of negotiations. Merlin then pulled out following fears of a property slump, and a planned 'Festival Marketplace' was deemed not fundable. A company called Rosehaugh came in to replace Merlin, and between them, they planned to make Brindley Place a thriving area throughout an almost 24-hour period. In October 1995, the canalside development won a top international honour award. The 'Excellence on the Waterfront' award was given to the City of Birmingham for the regeneration project at 'the Water's Edge', and Birmingham was the first British city to be presented with this award. A newspaper said, 'Landlocked Birmingham has shared the top honours with Boston and New York, in an international competition to find the world's best waterfronts. The city scooped the honour for the regeneration of the 200-year-old canalside around Gas Street Basin and Brindley Place. It includes 1,000 yards of waterfront with offices, restaurants, bars and shops.'

The International Convention Centre and Symphony Hall

Land for this was cleared in 1987, and it opened in 1991 at a cost of £180 million. This centre located next to Gas Street Basin comprises eleven halls, the largest of which is an exhibition hall that can seat 3,500. The National Indoor Arena, sited next to Birmingham's earliest canal junction (Old Turn) is specially designed for indoor athletics, and has been a regular venue for the TV *Gladiators* tournaments. The Hyatt Regency 314-bedroom, five-star hotel overlooks the site from the other side of the Gas Street Basin.

The National Sea Life Centre is also sited at Old Turn junction, opposite the NIA. In its first year of opening, the centre welcomed 1.5 million visitors to its underwater world, where the story of the River Severn, from stream to sea can be experienced.

At the end of the Birmingham wharves stood the BCN's company offices. Removed during the 1930s. (Birmingham Libraries)

9

A view of Gas Street Basin *c.* 1950, looking toward Broad Street Tunnel and the church that used to stand over it.

A closer look at Broad Street Tunnel during the 1960s. Charlie Foster takes a T. S. Element boat through Worcester Bar.

Gas Street Basin and Broad Street Tunnel in the distance in 2009.

Gas Street Basin during development. The James Brindley has now appeared, while other offices are in the throws of construction. The stub of canal once led through a bridge to the old wharves and company offices.

Just in front of what is now the James Brindley used to stand the warehouses belonging to the Severn & Canal Carrying Company. This photo shows them just prior to removal some time during the 1970s.

Residential apartments now occupy the space taken up by the Severn & CC warehouses, while a new cast-iron bridge in the style of the Horseley Iron Company has been erected over the Worcester Bar. The Cube is under construction at the turn of the Worcester Canal.

Above left and right: Gas Street, 1970s, looking from the bridge to the Old Wharves with Rail House in the distance, Broad Street Tunnel just around the corner to the right. (KH) The winter view from February 2010 focuses on the buildings next to Broad Street Tunnel. The church has long gone, while canal-sited buildings have all been cleaned up and now serve the public as bars and information places.

Looking across Gas Street Basin in 2008 to where the former two pictures were taken. The Hyatt Hotel now overlooks all.

Broad Street Tunnel during the 1970s before redevelopment.

2009. Convention Centre to the left and Brindley Place to the right and Broad Street Tunnel and Gas Street Basin in the distance.

Old Turn Junction during the 1970s before regeneration, with a very rundown towpath and Horseley Bridge. (KH) Below is the same view but a little further back to take in the new Malt House pub, where Bill Clinton once stood on the balcony, and a completely revitalised area outside the National Indoor Arena. The old brick bridge and the Horseley iron bridge have been well tended to.

A view up the Oozells Loop from the early twentieth century. Coal wharves used to occupy the space opposite the Sea Life Centre. The Oozells Loop today has modern apartments and office space, and there is no towpath access around this loop.

A view toward Farmers Bridge Top Lock, with Crescent Wharf just out of sight around the corner. It is interesting to see still horse-drawn boats as late as the 1970s. (KH) All of the dark smoke-stained walls have now been taken down, to be replaced by offices, but the building to the right has remained.

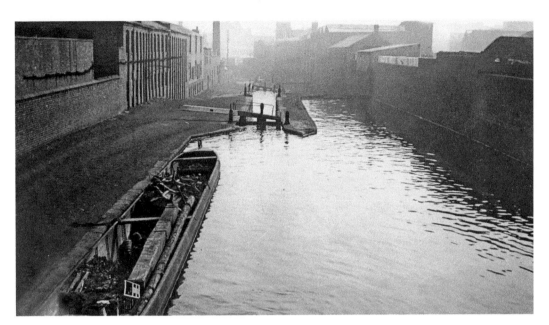

A closer view of Farmers Bridge Top Lock (*c.* 1950), and I know the picture is in sepia, but you can almost feel the dirt and grime. (WK) By 2009, the high brick walls have been replaced by clean modern buildings and a BT tower stands guard over all.

And just to show that some locations have remained pretty unaltered, this shot going down the Fazeley Canal and Farmers Bridge 13 is from the early twentieth century, as can be read from the garments of the ladies standing at the balance beam. Notice the horse eating from his nose can. (Pratt) The building over the bottom lock in the 2008 photograph is known as the 'Bothy'. Sorry, I don't know why, but it is only when you explore the canals for yourself that you come across such historical gems.

Main Line Canal

Smethwick, Winson Green through to West Bromwich

Leaving Birmingham behind and heading towards Wolverhampton, we soon come across two loops of the old Brindley Canal that were cut across when Telford created the new line during the late 1820s. Icknield Port Loop is the smaller southern loop but is important as a feeder from the Edgbaston reservoir. Water levels have been a vital topic over the last few years, with global warming prospects and also the expensive repairs to the Chasewater dam, which resulted in several canal activities being cancelled during 2010.

Throughout the years, canal pleasure trips have been popular. Boulton and Watt probably had the earliest extravagant trip when they took friends from Winson Green to the caverns at Tipton. In our photograph of the Winson Green Loop, we see a Sunday School outing using one of G. H. Rabones boats. Shortly following the loops, there are still some remains of the factory that Boulton and Watt used to manufacture parts for their steam engines, and the site is identified by a round brick chimney, though the basin that used to access the site is now closed off. After Smethwick junction, the two lines get very close to each other, and between them is a pumping station that used to take water from the lower level to top up the upper. It is not in operation today, but it has been recently restored from a derelict state, and the chimney has been rebuilt. It was reopened on Tuesday 14 November 2000, when an enthusiastic flock of canal and steam buffs, plus other interested individuals, herded themselves gently but eagerly into the Spartan bare-brick confines of the Smethwick pumping station. They were attentive to the mayor, Mrs Jean Marson, as she prepared to officially open the gleaming and freshly painted restoration. After a short speech, her gloved hand prodded a prominent green button on the wall and brought the glittering gold and silver metalwork of the engine and water pump to life. This glorious relic of the power of hot and hissing steam, plus its building and attendant chimney stack, has now become a welcome addition to the Galton Valley Heritage Centre of Smethwick.

The Galton Valley can easily be boated through and not appreciated for what it is. The only way to really understand and value this man-made valley is to stop and imagine the thousands of labourers slaving away with only picks, shovels and wheelbarrows. After going 70 feet to the level of the waterway, they then had to dig out the canal! These are some of the treasures that have been carried over from the canal age.

The pumping station is 118 years old to be precise. However, the restoration has, of necessity, introduced several cannibalised items, to regain a sense, feel and sound of what had been lost to neglect and the ravages of time. And to give credit where it is due, the parties concerned have made a laudable effort to present this historic package, with its racing-green castings and bright-red handrails. So what work has been undertaken to bring the water pumping station to something resembling its former glory?

Drifting back in time to 1892, we would have found the station newly erected and consisting of an unblemished utilitarian two-storey dark-blue brick exterior, a chimney stack twice its height, while inside sat two powerful steam engines prepared to lift thousands of gallons of dank water from the new to the old main line. The pumps were to replace the earlier Smethwick beam engines and satisfy the thirst of the upper and considerably older canal, by lifting water up 20 feet from the 453-foot to the 473-foot level. The engines were capable of moving 200 locks' worth per day. Brindley's old main line was, even at the close of the Victorian era, a busy canal, but its summit pound of less than two miles was continually drained of its precious water by the steady traffic passing through the Smethwick and Spon Lane locks.

The 1892 station had originally been supplied with two Lancashire boilers to provide steam that operated two sets of vertical crank compound engines, connected to 16-inch-diameter centrifugal pumps. Coal, the ubiquitous power of that generation, was delivered by the ton, straight from the narrow boats, moored only feet away, into the coal store. Unfortunately, the two original boilers, engines and pumps were lost after the closure of the station. By 1978, the station was derelict, all equipment had gone, the roof was in a bad way, the boiler room had become filled with canal dredgings, and the proud chimney that had been demolished during the 1930s had been shovelled into the building's ash pit. But also in that year (1978), the building received listed status, thus paving the way for eventual restoration. And so, over the ensuing eighteen years, in faltering but steady steps, the Smethwick pumping station was brought back to life. But where does one find pumps and boilers of this historic calibre?

Two Tangye pumps, similar to the originals, built at the famous Smethwick works in 1895, were discovered at Wallsend Slipway & Dry Dock Company, and Tyneside Metropolitan Borough Council did the decent thing and donated them to the project. One of these engines, along with its pump was subsequently installed into the station's main hall, while its companion went to Birmingham Science Museum. The replacement boiler has come from much closer quarters, originating from Rolfe Street Baths, just down the road near Smethwick's High Street. This colossal 30-ton, cast-iron cylindrical boiler, 30 feet long and with a diameter of 9 feet, was installed after much puffing and panting in 1989. The next stage of the project was the reconstruction of the chimney stack, and the building of that began in the same year after carefully studying photographs by P. C. Richardson of Middlesbrough. Constructed with traditional red and blue Staffordshire engineering bricks, the new chimney is 83 feet tall, cost £102,000, and was completed in 1990.

The pumping station was now starting to take shape, and in 1992, the contractors, William Gough and Dorothea Restorations, came along to do more work to internal components.

Dorothea Restorations are probably the country's leading experts when dealing with historical engineering reconstructions. With some twenty-five years practical experience, their consultants and engineers have acquired a unique combination of specialist skills after being engaged in an intimate way with a wide variety of restoration projects. Over that quarter of a century, their work has included the restoration of bridges, windmills and steam locomotives, and they were called to Smethwick for their specialist knowledge, thus completing work to the engine and pump.

Later on, the coal storage hole was dug out, and an external wall rebuilt, and finally, after a successful lottery bid, the finishing touches were made early in 2000 in preparation for the grand opening.

West Bromwich

Pudding Green and Bromford Junction are both found on the Birmingham Main Line Canal about halfway between Birmingham and Wolverhampton, and both were created when Telford brought the new canal through in the late 1820s. But Pudding Green – what an evocative name for a junction. Certainly you couldn't buy a pudding for love nor money, nor have there ever been any pudding factories at this location –nor even a green. But take a look at the accompanying map and you will spy several clay pits, for in the nineteenth and early twentieth centuries, there were many brick manufactories in this area, requiring massive clay extraction. So perhaps in the canal construction days, clay from here was used to puddle the canals – hence the name. On that map, you will see the early Wednesbury canal coming from the top of the diagram, doing a curve by Izon's Foundry, and then going east to Birmingham. The new Telford canal then cuts across the old line and goes from left to right. Several new junctions with the old canal were formed where old and new canals intersected. The cut-off curve became known as Izon's Turn, and a boatyard sprang up between the waterways.

The new line formed a second junction a short distance away by cutting through the 'Union' or Roway Branch. This served the Union Colliery and Union Furnaces, where girders for many BCN road bridges were manufactured. It was abandoned – like so many others in 1955, and built over with little trace of its existence. The Izon Branch just north of the junction was named after the West Bromwich iron founder, who along with a business partner had started out at Greet Mill. As mentioned earlier, West Bromwich had a thriving brick industry, and Piercy Brickworks (noticeable by its row of kilns) was advantageously placed right next to the canal; narrow boats were perfect for shifting tons of bricks. Like many other companies, it dug its own small branch for wharfage, and a small side bridge still marks the spot today. The Piercy works was run as a partnership between Joseph Hamblet and Mr Parkes, who utilised part of J. E. Piercy's estate through to the 1860s, when Hamblet became the sole proprietor.

During the 1870s and 1880s, this busy company was producing blue and red bricks, flooring and roofing tiles, paving, kerbs and many other articles, though blue bricks were always their speciality.

Edgbaston reservoir, with Birmingham in the distance. This is one of the vital water supplies to the BCN.

Outing from Winson Green. Early twentieth century. (Joe Safe) Very few boats come this way today, though it is an interesting loop to explore. All of the early housing has gone.

The site of Boulton & Watt's mint and engine works.

Smethwick. The 1769 Brindley line on the left and Telford line to the right, separated only by the embankment. The difference in levels at this point is 20 feet.

The brass works has long gone, being replaced by housing, as has the second of the two Smethwick top locks, though the top canal is much hidden by the general greening of the landscape.

A close look at Smethwick top lock, with a boat coming off the Engine Arm.

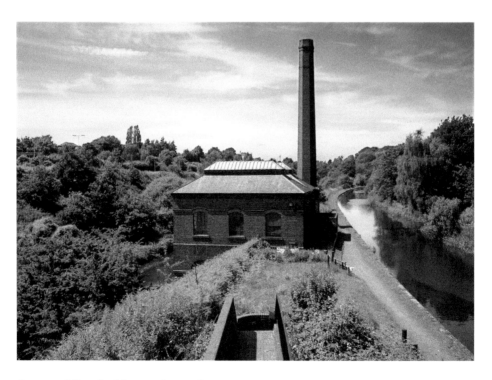

A restored Smethwick pumping station, 2010.

Sandwell Park Colliery brought its coal along a rail track to the busy West Bromwich wharf on the Old Main Line *c.* 1940. (Sandwell Libraries) The BCN Society has recently placed an information board at the location.

Old main line coal chutes for the Sandwell Park Colliery still in operation during the 1970s. (KH)

Above and left: Looking towards Spon Lane top lock from Spon Lane Bridge sometime during the 1960s. (DW) Radical changes have taken place along Spon Lane locks since then. All of the engineering works on the right have gone, and the canal was realigned to accommodate the construction of the M5, which opened in 1970.

One of Thomas Clayton's gas boats, with Jack Taylor, sits in Spon Lane top lock, probably during the 1940s. (DTD) The modern image of the top lock looks in the other direction.

Spon Lane locks, *c.* 1950. This is the middle lock, with top lock in the distance. There was very little development on the left bank, but a hive of industry around top lock. (WK) There is now an industrial estate on the left, M5 in the distance, and a factory unit making flooring to the right, though this suffered a severe fire in early 2010. Blackberries now grow abundantly on the left bank and I pick them in September for pies.

Main line canal, West Bromwich. T. S. Elements boats – tug in front, loaded with coal, 1960s. (DW)

Main line canal, West Bromwich, looking towards Dudley Port with a horse-drawn coal boat, 1960s. The Gulf terminal has gone, as have the brickworks chimneys in the distance. Note the boat is equipped with a pump to stop it sinking. (DW)

Pudding Green Junction, mid-twentieth century, where the Wednesbury Old Canal (WOC) leaves the new main line. From this map, one can see how the WOC comes from Wednesbury (top left) and then curves before heading away to Spon lane Junction. The later Telford Canal cut across, forming a loop. A short cut that existed until the middle of the twentieth century can also be seen between the two lines and served Albion Ironworks. The loop, which served Izon's foundry, also had a busy boatbuilding yard at one stage, while the Izon Branch and arm into Piercy Brickworks have been filled in. West Bromwich was a busy town for brickworks in the early twentieth century, and two, along with their clay pits, can be seen on this map. Old pit shafts are dotted about the map and are typical of all maps of the Black Country during this period.

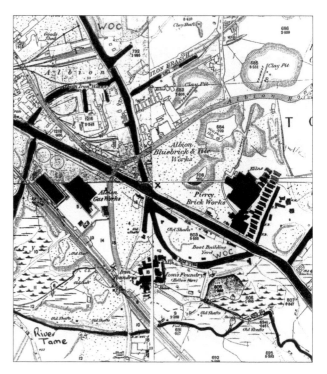

Don't be fooled by the working boat. This shot along the main line is from 2010.

Tipton

During the fifteenth and sixteenth centuries Tipton was just another little Hamlet, but by the eighteenth century, the several small communities of Tipton Green, Tibbington, Toll End, Ocker Hill, Burnt Tree, Horseley Heath and Great Bridge, were growing, as industrialisation started to make an impact. However, it was the arrival of the Birmingham Canal that powered the dynamic expansion and cohesion of Tipton and influenced the development of its primary centre. For not only was Tipton right in the middle of the route between Wolverhampton and Birmingham, it also sat at the centre of the productive 30-foot coal seam that defined the area that came in time to be known as the Black Country. Yes, the Black Country was not named after the soot and smoke that it produced in vast quantities, but from this geological black stuff that had been sitting quietly under its turf for some millions of years. Coal, iron ore, limestone and clay were to turn Tipton and its neighbours into the industrial heartland of Britain. Continuing for a hundred years from 1769 onwards, Tipton received its own network of canals, arms and basins, to serve the growing number of coal mines, ironworks, brick manufactories and associated industrial appendages connected with all that activity.

Within its misshapen 3 miles by 2, that is to say, approximately 5 square miles, there came to be 13 ½ miles of man-made waterway. They were 4 ¼ miles of Old Main Line, 2 miles of new main line, 1 ¼ miles of the Walsall Canal, plus 6 miles of branches. And that's not counting many smaller basins.

In addition to coal mining and the making of iron, Tipton developed its heavy engineering trades, which include the production of castings, forgings, structural ironwork, steam engines, boilers, chains and anchors. In 1825, the Horseley Ironworks built the world's first iron steam ship (*Aaron Manby*), and in 1829, Telford's Galton Bridge. In 1843, the Gospel Oak Ironworks made the cast-iron columns for the Albert Dock in Liverpool, which are now part of a listed building. In 1856, the firm of H. P. Parkes built what was then the world's largest anchor for Brunel's steamship the *Great Eastern*. It is not surprising that Tipton was described by the well-known Midland historian F. W. Packwood as 'palpitating with the beat and throb of a thousand engines'.

Work in any of the industries at this time was a dangerous affair, and perhaps the most dangerous of all was mining the coal seams. In 1849, there was a particularly tragic accident at the 'Blue Fly Pit' at Dudley Port, where sixteen men and boys lost their lives. In 1851, a large piece of coal was sent from Tipton to the Great Exhibition in London. After being raised from the Denbigh Colliery at a depth of 495 feet, and weighing a massive 13 tons, it was cut by Round's Colliery at Tividale into a smooth cylinder weighing 6 tons. It was polished until it resembled jet. I think that this case alone demonstrates the importance of coal and also the pride of its extractors in that mineral.

Many different kinds of boats plied the Tipton Canals. In addition to the slow plod of single-class goods (i.e., loaded with one commodity, such as coal), there were fly boats that travelled at a good trot, and horses were changed at regular intervals, just as post horses in a chaise journey. Those fly boats were all timed at regular intervals along the route, just as buses and trains are today, and their hulls were designed to pass through the water much more efficiently. Also, there were the packet boats, designed and scheduled to carry passengers only. In 1851, Swift Packets, run by Thomas Monk of Tipton, were carrying passengers from Wolverhampton to Birmingham via Tipton in two hours and ten minutes for one shilling. The now-famous firm of Fellows, Morton & Clayton had its beginnings in 1837 next door to Tipton, in West Bromwich, by James Fellows. He started to concentrate on the long-distance trade and by 1855 was taking as much as 13,000 tons of iron from the Birmingham area down to London. As the business continued to grow, he moved his base of operations to Toll End in Tipton, then describing himself as a canal and railway carrier.

This photograph from the early twentieth century has been used many times by writers including myself, but it is just so wonderful. Here we have a family working for the Shropshire Union Canal Carrying Co. taking a break right next to the Fountain pub in the heart of Tipton. Notice the crates and barrels that are being carried. Amazingly, the house in the middle distance is still there, and probably one of the oldest in Tipton. Taken from across the canal by the new Neptune Health Centre, the modern photo looks at the curved wall where the previous family are seated. The wall hasn't changed and you can still sit on it today. The Fountain pub also shows some early brickwork at the rear. 2008 was an important date in Tipton's canal calendar. It was the first year that they organised a modern working-boat festival. The sun shone and a good time was had by all. (KH)

Working boats on display, September 2008. (KH)

Ocker Hill Power Station cooling towers dominated the skies in Tipton through to 1987, when it was demolished for a new housing estate. (KH) Below is the Tames Valley Junction today – 2010.

This time a horse-drawn boat sets the scene passing the curving bulk of the towers in 1967. (DW) A new housing estate has taken the place of the coal-fired power station in 2009, while few boats now venture along this low pound of the Walsall Canal.

On the canal bank by the power station, as coal boats each year deliver thousands of tons of coal, *c.* 1950. (KH)

The WOC, not far from Pudding Green Junction and two of T. Clayton's boats head for Oldbury in 1965. (DW) Buildings come and buildings go in this same location.

Walsall Canal at Ocker Hill. This is the short Ocker Hill branch that served as a source of water for the Ocker Hill engines that lay on the hill some few hundred yards away. Up to the second half of the twentieth century, there were literally hundreds of coal yards throughout the system; this wharf was operated by Marsters. Today, this short arm is a secure mooring for a handful of residential boaters; BW used to have their headquarters here but moved out in around 2005.

Great Bridge, *c.* 1965, and a horse boat takes a break almost at the bottom of the Ryder's Green locks. Across the bridge was the large firm of Wellington Tube. Wellington Tube has been replaced by JJB Sports and ASDA, while the bridge has been remodelled somewhat.

Great Bridge, with Ryder's Green locks in the distance and Wellington Tube on the left as we approach the bridge from the other direction. The horse boat is probably Caggy Steven's rubbish boat, *c.* 1966 (DW) A new footbridge across to ASDA is now in evidence, with the Ryder's Green locks now more visible.

The bottom lock of Ryder's Green locks complete with lock house and stabling facilities. The entrance to the now-defunct Haines Branch was beyond the horse. The bottom lock in 2010 is a very different scene.

Oldbury

When Brindley's canal came through Oldbury in 1772, it, like many of the other now-well-established towns like West Bromwich and Tipton, was just a collection of hamlets and farms. Industrial output, if it could be called that, was provided by a small group of forges, which later became 'The Brades'. Our map from 1857 shows considerably development around the canal loop after almost ninety years. The modern town centre is in evidence inside the loop, while a later cutting has encircled the town. We can see many basins and wharves serving the furnaces and a burgeoning chemical industry that is growing to the west of the town. The loop, or town arm as it was known, disappeared during the 1960s following the demise of those industries, and the land was redeveloped. But there are still a few hints at its existence, and of course a handful of photographs. Tube making took off in Oldbury following the invention of lap-welded tube by Cornelius Whitehouse in 1825, and this cheaper tube sped up the ability to use coal gas lighting. The tubing industry grew rapidly.

The chemical industry started in 1835 when the Chance brothers set up a plant for making raw materials for their glass-making works at Spon Lane, West Bromwich. This later became Chance & Hunt, and it was soon followed by Albright & Wilson, who moved to Oldbury in the 1850s. The boats of Thomas Clayton were already at work carrying by-products from the early gasworks, and when the Demuth tar works was set up in Oldbury in 1865, Clayton boats were soon contracting for them. Later, the company moved much closer to Demuth, where they occupied property between Tat Bank Ironworks and the junction to the Titford Canal. They operated their distinctive 'gas' boats right up to 1965, when manufactured gas had had its day. The Demuth company later became the Midland Tar Distillery, and Clayton's delivered many thousands of gallons of crude tar from some 150 gasworks, to be distilled into other products. For example, MTD produced pyridine, a basic raw material of sulphonamide drugs. Pyridine is also used in the dyestuffs industry for denaturing alcohol and for making fabrics crease proof. Crude tar became one of the raw materials for synthetic resins, solvents such as toluole, xylole, and the naphthas used in paints and varnishes. Toluole is a raw material used in the manufacture of saccharin and explosives – only don't get the two mixed up when you make your tea. Creosote, another of the materials that Clayton's regularly transported, was much used for timber preservation and also the foundation for disinfectants.

Arthur Albright first made phosphorus at Birmingham in 1844, and a few years later, 'The Phosphorus Works' of Albright & Wilson was established in Oldbury. In 1844, phosphorus was only a chemical curiosity; it was difficult to deal with because of its inflammability and the disease that accompanied its manufacture. Nevertheless, a year or so later, a less flammable form of phosphorus was made on a larger scale. Albright & Wilson's exhibit of it as a novelty at the Great Exhibition of 1851 marked the start of the modern match industry. Albright & Wilson went on to play a leading part in the chemical industry.

Titford Pump House

The building known as the pump house was used to recirculate water up the Titford locks and was part of a much greater collection of pumps around the BCN to control water supplies. It is, in fact, a series of buildings that have been added to and adapted as canal technology changed. Initially, it was a single tall engine room with a second tall engine room being added when more pumping power was needed. This resulted in the twin building we see today. The lean-to building at the side of the one engine room was built later to house a blacksmith shop. The boiler house at the rear was probably built and then enlarged when the second engine room was built. The pump house has recently been restored (2002) and is now an excellent base for the Birmingham Canal Navigations Society, and is regenerating use of the Titford Canal (511 feet). With the society now centring its activities more firmly on the Titford Canal, it is hoped that it will prosper.

Map of Oldbury, 1835, showing the town arm, industries arms and basins. The town arm was filled in after the 1960s, as was the long wharf know simply as 'the chemical arm' (Houghton Arm) that served the Alkali Works. (DTD)

A shot probably during the late 1950s from Whimsey Bridge with the Alkali Works in the distance. There were many arms off to the right, while the eastern entrance to the town arm was under the bridge on the left, just beyond the houses lining the canal towpath. The carriers T. S. Elements used to have a yard to the right, which later became Allen's yard, for boat repairs. Here we see a horse-drawn boat carrying what looks like timber. (DTD) The view from Whimsey Bridge in 2010 shows A and E Aquatics, who initially started with tropical and marine fish, but now supply everything to do with gardens and ponds. A couple of the shorter old arms can still be seen in the distance.

Allen's yard, with at least two of Elements' boats in for repair. (H. Foster)

This is a view along the town arm, not far from the bridge in the earlier photo. Mecca Bingo now occupies the slot. In view is Ratcliffe's ironworks. Oldbury had an engineering industry that supplied carriage wheels for the railways. (DTD)

Clayton boat at the junction with the Titford Canal. (DTD)

Thomas Clayton's yard during their final decade of activity during the 1960s. (DTD) The photo below shows Oldbury Junction in the distance beyond the concrete bridge, while Clayton's yard was on the right. Now everything is under the shadow of the mighty M5 since 1970.

The Titford pump house during the rundown years of the 1970s. (KH) Today, the pump house has been lovingly restored and now serves admirably as the headquarters for the BCN Society with its meetings and functions, including the annual boat gathering, 2010.

Above left: Just a short way along the Titford Canal from the pump house is Langley Maltings, a wonderful building that was badly burned early in 2009. This is a photo of restoration during the 1970s. (KH)

Above right: Langley Maltings during the 2009 boat gathering at the pump house.

Part of the Old Town arm that ran under West Bromwich Street. (KH)

Looking towards High Bridge, Oldbury, with the firm of Accles & Pollack's on the left. T. & S. Elements were big coal carriers right through to the 1960s; they had a second depot at Salford. (KH) New industrial units have replaced Accles & Pollack's, while fishermen now take advantage of cleaner water – and fish.

Brades middle lock, Oldbury. The area across the lock was a small dairy farm with about twenty cattle through to the middle of the twentieth century. In the 1940s, it was rented to Mr and Mrs Monk, who used the building on the left as the cattle shed. Ruth Collins, who lived at the lock cottage with her father Will King, remembers the dwelling house on the right as a substantial building with a grand oak staircase. A haha encircled the house to prevent the cattle straying. Two cottages used to be just along the towpath; each had only one room, and the occupants drew a curtain to make a bedroom. One can just see the edge of a rather large oil tank which was here in the 1970s. (KH) Now, the farm has gone, and beyond the trees sits a rather lavishly ornamented Hindu temple.

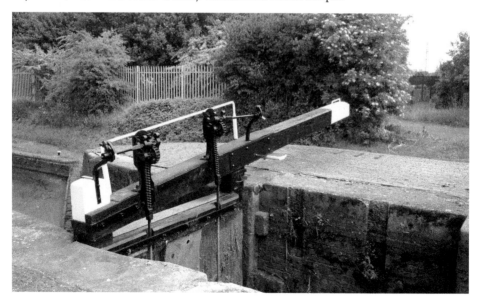

Dudley and Stourbridge Canals

Just as there is a perceptible change of dialect between Black Country towns, so there is a different feel to the canals west of the Rowley ridge. The two Dudley canals became part of the BCN family in 1846, though the Stourbridge never did succumb, and due to the convoluted nature of the land as it tumbles haphazardly toward the Severn Valley, these three waterways have a charm that the rest of the BCN does not possess. That is probably why the two major Midland canal festivities are held at either Park Head, Dudley, or Bumble Hole, Netherton. The weather was fabulous in August 2008 at Park Head, and I went along for the show and to take some photographs. With a gathering of historic boats and engines, stalls, steam engines, horse-drawn boat, craft exhibits, model boats and much more, hundreds turned out to enjoy the two-day event. Meanwhile, happy sightseers cruised off south along the Dudley No. 1 Canal on the trip boat *Electra*.

Less than a hundred years ago, the area was thick with collieries, clay pits, ironworks and furnaces, but now it is a perfect venue for showing the working boats off to advantage. Again, there was good support from the IWA, BCNS society, Dudley Canal Trust, and other volunteers who made everything run smoothly. Members of the Black Country Living Museum also made a good showing, and dressed up in period costume to add that special flavour to the event.

The Dudley No. 1 canal runs from a connection with the Tipton canals at Tipton Junction, via the 3,154-yard Dudley Tunnel, to an end-on connection with the Stourbridge at the bottom of the Delph flight of locks, which were improved and straightened in 1858. The Stourbridge locks, on the other hand, have a much more irregular way of coping with the landscape. A stroll along the Stourbridge locks is a very satisfying way of passing an hour or two, and probably the most striking feature of that walk would be the Red House Cone, a large bottle-shaped kiln. Made of brick, and 100 feet high, it belonged to Stuart Crystal, one of the famous glass-making names from the past, and one of the last to disappear.

The Red House Cone has been well preserved as a tribute to the early Stourbridge glass trade, but in former days, there were more than a dozen in the area, and they made a striking feature to the landscape. This was the time when Stourbridge was one of the leading towns for glass production in Britain. Like many industries of the eighteenth and nineteenth centuries, the glass industry has almost disappeared, but the account of its arrival and glory days has not been forgotten. The story of the Stourbridge glass industry is one of religious persecution, hard sweated toil, child labour, secret skills and recipes, and later an intimate relationship with the Stourbridge canal that made it grow tenfold. Of course, the glass industry predated the Stourbridge canal of 1779 by some 150 years. But as with other industries, the glass makers, dependent on a poor road system, were quick to promote, fund and utilise the new canal system at its inception. So how did glass making come to be in the heart of the Midlands in the first place?

During the Middle Ages, the best glass came from Europe, but when religious persecution came in the early seventeenth century, coupled with financial incentives from England, several families decided to come here, especially those residing in Lorraine. At first, they settled in the Forest of Dean, but due to rapidly disappearing timber – the fuel for glassmakers, brewers, metalworkers, lime burners and the manufacturers of tar, starch, sugar and a host of other industries – they had to move on. Forests were disappearing at a worrying rate, and the government had to legislate against the cutting down of trees. In the Midlands, coal was being tested as a substitute for wood, and Dud Dudley discovered a method of using coal that didn't ruin the iron. Enter Paul Tyzack.

Paul Tyzack was a young master of glass making in the early 1600s; his family had been using the art for at least two hundred years. He heard of the successful use of coal in furnaces and came to the Stourbridge area. In the second decade of the seventeenth century, Stourbridge was a busy market town in the parish of Oldswinford, standing on the banks of the River Stour. It had a population of around 500 people supporting a thriving trade in leather and cloth; and with Paul Tyzack, the glass men arrived. Not only did he find abundant supplies of coal, he also discovered a local clay, in fact, the best clay he had ever come across for making his pots. Pots were an essential part of the glassmaker's work. About three feet high and with thick walls, they sat at the heart of the furnace. Raw materials for the glass were placed into the pots and the molten glass was later gathered from the hole at the top. Native glassmakers to Stourbridge were probably making small green vessels and phials; Paul was here to make window glass.

Glass Cones

The brick-built cones, towering 100 feet above the landscape, performed a dual function. Ultimately, the structure was a simple chimney, designed to create great flows of air through the centrally located furnace, thus maintaining the high temperatures necessary to melt the glass. But, opened out at the base, it provided the area for the glassmakers to perform their art. Inside, the atmosphere was hot, smoky and full of noise, as the teams of men – organised into 'chairs' – worked in shifts in order to keep the furnaces hot day and night.

The glass trade was always hungry for coal, and mines littered the area, but brick-making also became important along the Dudley and Stourbridge canal system, both for general construction, and also for kiln-making. One of the earliest forms to gain success in the early nineteenth century with fire brick manufacture was Messrs Perrins & Harrison of Lye. It later came under the control of Mr George King Harrison, who came to be locally known as the king of clay. He extended the operations to Brettell Lane and nearby Nagersfield, where the company's colliery was reputed to contain one of the finest seams of Old Mine clay in the world.

The mined clay was taken from the pithead to weathering grounds, where it was graded by skilled 'sorters' and where it then lay for a considerable time. This was essential for the clay, when later fired, to cope with the intense heat within the furnace. Harris & Pearson, also of Brettell Lane, gained a global reputation and claimed to be one of the oldest established and largest firms of Fire Bricks and Gas Retort manufacturers. It was first established at Amblecote Old Works in 1739 and worked for more than 100 years, before being bought by Harris & Pearson in the 1840s. An initial six-acre site became too small, and they built a new nine-acre site in 1870.

A description of the operations reads, 'The Clay is brought from the pits and first picked by women who have been carefully trained. Clay for glass house pots undergoes further scrutiny to screen out any impurities. Later it is crushed into powder, sieved and then mixed with water and moulded generally by women. After the bricks had been dried, they were then taken to the kilns.' The company's advertising blurb then stated that 'the bricks were stamped 'Harris and Pearson' and dispatched to every civilised country of the globe'. They were proud of their fire bricks, as were Messrs E. J. & J. Pearson Limited, whose firm also lined the canal banks off Brettell Lane. They also carried on the manufacture of Stourbridge firebricks and fireclay goods at the Delph Works, and the Crown Works, Amblecote. The business was founded in the year 1860, and an important and wide-reaching connection was built up. In 1872, the late Mr J. W. Thomas joined the firm, which continued to develop its business, and in 1898, it was converted into a private limited company, under the present name of E. J. & J. Pearson Limited.

Bumble Hole, Netherton, is the other fabulous Dudley venue for boat gatherings, and the rambling green hillside, with its vacant but potent symbol of steam power, Cobb's Engine House, simply reverberates with the echoes of long-lost industries. In the nineteenth and early twentieth centuries, this was a dirty place of mines and iron works, though everyone must admit that, as Warren's Hall Nature Reserve, it has cleaned up nicely. It's just a little sad that the visitor centre was burned out in May 2010. Fire crews from Dudley attended the blaze but much of the building was damaged. Unfortunately, I don't have a photograph from the past, but I do have one from the Homer Hill pit, which shows just how Warren's Hall Colliery No. 3 and the engine house would have looked.

Our map of the area shows the Dudley No. 2 canal coming in from the left, from its wanderings around Netherton church. It does a tight loop around Sir Horace St Paul's land with its Windmill End ironworks, before going east to its junction with the Worcester & Birmingham Canal via Gosty and Lapal tunnels. When the Netherton Tunnel was dug in 1855, the loop was cut across, but by this time, the pumping engine was already installed and working. It proved to have a double purpose, and as Michael Pearson said so well in his guidebook to the Stourport Ring, the pump kept the mines dry and the cut wet.

And to complete our look at the charismatic and well-loved Dudley canals, we close with a look at the Netherton Tunnel of 1858. This tunnel has well been described as the jewel in the crown of the BCN, but there is never any room for complacency because the tunnel has failed at least twice in its recent history and been closed off. British Waterways engineers monitor the tunnel's walls at least once a month for any movement, and we all fervently hope that the tunnel will stay open for a long time.

The first image shows a glass cone in the early twentieth century in Stourbridge. The glass cone of Stuart Crystal, seen in both the 1950s (KH) and 2010, has now been revitalised as an education and visitors centre.

Above left: Glass worker, inside one of the cones, early twentieth century. (Broadfield Glass Museum Kingswinford)

Above right: Walking down the Stourbridge locks toward the glass cone. Dadford's Shed in the middle ground. (Infrared shot by R. Horton)

Display cabinet at Broadfield Museum showing some of the beautiful glass made in the Stourbridge area.

Blowers Green Lock is seen in 1934, with workers rebuilding the lock. (WK) By the time of the Canal Festival in 2008, the former blue-brick building was the home to the Dudley Canals Trust.

Right: Boats and people making their way up the Park Head locks.

Below: Well-maintained working boats, associated stalls and historic vehicles all make for an entertaining day in 2008.

At Brettell Lane Brick Manufactories, Stourbridge Canal, Messrs E. J. & J. Pearson Limited carry on the manufacture of Stourbridge firebricks and fireclay goods at the Delph Works, and the Crown Works, Amblecote. (CM) Little evidence of the mighty brickworks remains today, and a modern trading estate now occupies the area along the canal bank.

The Delph Works, early twentieth century. The area was called Black Delph because of its coal and dirt. (CM) In the modern image, opposite where the Delph Works used to be, a modern housing estate is now sited on the land.

The Homer Hill pit, which would be very similar to that of Bumble Hole during the late nineteenth and early twentieth centuries. (CM)

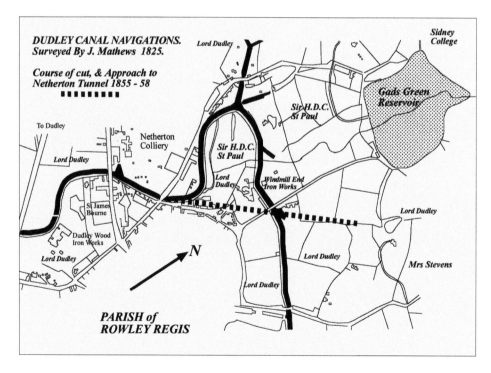

Map of Bumble Hole, the Dudley No. 2 Canal, and the plan for the Netherton Tunnel cut – dotted line. The loop is known as the Boshboil Arm, and there are still sections of it left today.

Above left and right: A pencil drawing of the pumping house and its ancillary buildings as it would have appeared in the early twentieth century. (Drawing by Jane Davies.) In 2010, the empty engine house, with its attendant stack, stares across the sloping landscape toward the distant Clent Hills.

Miners at work in one of the Dudley mines. (CM)

Looking toward the entrance of the southern portal of the Netherton Tunnel. With the visitor centre to the right and a trio of Toll End iron bridges at the junction, Windmill End is a fabulous location.

Above left and right: A boat gathering at Windmill End in 2008, at the celebration of the 150th year of the opening of the Netherton Tunnel.

In the foreground of this image of the Dudley Tunnel is Dr John Fletcher of Wednesbury (1934-96) who founded the Dudley Canal Tunnel Preservation Society (later the Dudley Canal Trust) in 1964 and co-founded, with John Brimble of Tipton, the Black Country Society in 1967. He is undoubtedly the most influential figure in recent times in the battle to ensure that the history, achievements and identity of the Black Country became recognised and appreciated. (KH) Below, a boat gathering is underway at the Dudley Tunnel portal, Park Head, in 2008.

The Tipton end of the tunnel with an Alfred Matty boat, *c.* 1968. I love this picture because it has the old sign showing that the tunnel was 3,027 yards. This was taken away and replaced with an unmentionable number of metres. (DW)

Even earlier, a horse-drawn Clayton boat (*Mole?*) about to go through in 1955. (WK)

Repairs to the tunnel during 1983 with a Caggy Stevens boat in evidence. The tunnel was reopened after extensive concrete sections to the canal bed had been inserted, by Sir Frank Price on 17 April 1984.

This page: Tipton end of the tunnel during the 1970s. (GW) At the 2008 celebrations of the tunnel's 150th opening, dignitaries gather at the Tipton end while the band takes five minutes at the Netherton end.

Coomb's Wood basin early twentieth century with Gosty Hill tunnel portal in the distance. (Pratt)

Hawne Basin seen in the 1960s (DW) and in 2008, now home to many leisure boats.

Looking down the Delph eight locks, 1950s, with all of the industry of Black Delph in sight at the bottom. The arm to the left shows the line of the original locks before the improvements of the mid-1800s. (KH) A greening of the landscape as an Alvechurch boat with holidaymakers heads toward Stourbridge in 2010.

Walsall

Walsall at one time was the town for leather production, and a few small companies still specialise in saddles. Today, a leather museum sits comfortably at the heart of the town to continue to tell the historic story. The story of the town's canals, however, commenced in great rivalry between two contending groups. One group, which met at Warwick in 1770, promoted a plan of taking a canal from Walsall to Fradley via Lichfield. The powerful Birmingham Company didn't like that scheme at all, and in the end, they made a start towards the town by cutting a line from the Wednesbury canal at Ryder's Green (West Bromwich) to Broadwaters (Moxley). And finally, after more wrangling, the Birmingham Company extended the line from Broadwaters around Darlaston and into Walsall, by June 1799.

As far as the twentieth century is concerned, no one knows the Walsall canals better than Jack Haddock, who was an energetic eighty-something in 2009. Jack didn't purposely set out to catalogue the final days of the working boat around Walsall, but that is what he did with his camera from the 1930s through to the 1970s. Jack still rides his bicycle to the Walsall History centre most weeks, but his contribution to the film data stored at that location in Essex Street is enormous. Towards the end of the Second World War, it dawned on him that the industrial world of horse-drawn boats and belching smoke stacks was disappearing fast. Jack describes one of his earliest memories:

> One of my earliest memories of Walsall is of a view from the balcony of a Corporation tramcar, as it rose over the steep hump of a narrow canal bridge en route to Bloxwich. As you approached the bridge, there was the majestic sight of Pratt's Flour Mill with its imposing height and numerous small windows covered in flour dust. Down below on the canal I saw a number of finely painted narrow boats unloading sacks of wheat. Opposite the mill was a small turnover bridge leading to Peter Keay & Sons boat dock.
>
> A continual relay of horse-drawn boats visited Pratt's Mill, but in the late 1930s, tugs began to appear towing a butty each. The horse would be accommodated at Keay's at the charge of 6 pence per night. I remember one boat staying moored for several days while the boatman's wife had a baby. Prior to the Second World War, Pratt's Mill was taken over by Price's bread, which worked at full capacity during the desperate days of the war. One nightly ritual was the fitting of stop planks under the bridge by the local Civil Defence force – just in case the canal happened to be bombed by the Luftwaffe. Work rapidly dropped off after the war's end, and the mill's working life came to an abrupt end with a disastrous fire in 1952, and as with many stretches of canal, this place has sadly lost its character.

The mid-1930s was a period stricken with unemployment, so government improvement schemes included the renewal of Pratt's Mill Bridge. The new Pratt's Mill Bridge was one of a number that were widened for burgeoning road transport. On the west side of the bridge were two coal wharves belonging to H. S. Thomas, and Bunch & Co. respectively; both owned their own narrow boats and also operated horse-drawn drays for home delivery. Jack's first camera was a Kodak box type, and then later a slightly better Zeiss Nettar for £20, which was a lot of money in 1954, before moving on to a Pentax Spotmatic -35mm. He continued photographing the changes happening in the Walsall area. The old boat companies were shutting one by one after the Second World War, but Jimmy Yates carried on in Lime Lane, Pelsall, for some years, as did Ken Keay, who as late as 1968 built a boat for H. F. Truman, who still operate boats today for young people. One of the great canal characters of the past was Ernie Thomas, who ran a large boat company and lived next to Walsall locks, just above Walsall Flour Mill. Nevertheless, the day of the working boat had come to its natural end on the BCN, and Thomas had the contract to scrap many of them. Jack remembers that, in 1934, a flying circus came to town, and Ernie treated his boatmen to a flight for 5s each. Ah – them was the days.

Pelsall and the Wyrley & Essington

We finish off with a look at winter working on the Wyrley & Essington Canal at Pelsall during the 1950s, when the ice-breaking team had to go out so that the working boats could carry on with their deliveries. So, imagine the scene: an early frosty morning in the January of 1954 around Pelsall Common. Snow has been falling for some days and has blanketed the canal and surrounding land. Ice on the cut is already over an inch thick. Nevertheless, the coal boat crews still have a job to do – to get their coal from the pits around Cannock to the waiting wharves. Some coal companies like Leonard Leigh and Alfred Matty had tugs that were capable of breaking a road through the ice, as long as it wasn't too thick. Other boats must wait until the company ice boat has gone through; so they wait patiently, shivering in the hatches until they can get underway.

Suddenly they hear a zinging and cracking noise coming from the ice around them which heralds the arrival of the strange hardy craft. Around the towpath come four sweating horses with hot breath pounding from their nostrils. Some fifty or sixty yards behind them comes the ice boat; heavy timbers covered with metal sheeting, while the crew of about eight overcoated men frantically rock the boat from side to side as they crack the ice beneath the battered hull. The horses and boat are past in a moment, and this is the time for the waiting crews to follow in the wake. It's back to work again.

This was the scene day after day on the BCN and Britain's canals during the winter months, though as we can see from this wonderful collection of photographs from Kathleen Cox, on the Curley Wyrley, they turned to using tractors.

James Williams, Kathleen's father, started out as a miner in the Cannock pits during the 1920s, before transferring to the Canal Company sometime in the 1940s. In that decade, he joined one of the maintenance gangs that roamed the BCN doing everything from repairing puddling to hedge cutting. And during the winter, he joined the ice-boat team, and Kathleen remembers her father coming home on many a winter's night cold and soaked through after cutting roads through the ice and snow.

The bottom of the Walsall locks with the Town Arm to the right and Flour Mill above the lock on the main road (not Pratt's) *c.* 1970. (KH)

One of the early boat rallies later on during the 1970s. (KH)

A redeveloped area around the junction, 2010.

This page: Looking up the town arm, early in the 1970s (JH) and a little later in that decade. (KH) In 2009, we are still waiting for Walsall to develop the arm. A very utilitarian box-style art gallery sits at the end of the arm.

Looking down Walsall locks
toward the town junction, 1970s.
(KH) In 2008, a redeveloped flour
mill and upmarket apartments
can be seen.

A view up Walsall locks with a horse-drawn boat and again in 2009. In the early 1970s, Ken Keay and Caggy Stevens had one of the last contracts to deliver pipes for the distribution of natural gas. (JH)

Walsall top lock with a gate repair in 1934 (WK) and in 2009.

A view of Sneyd Junction in the 1960s, with ice-breaker in the foreground and old cars in the maintenance yard – as was. (WK) In 2005, the BCN cottages have gone and the maintenance yard is now home to residential boats.

Catshill Junction (behind) with the toll house in front. (WK)

Tractors preparing to haul the ice boat. The boat appears to be of timber construction and BCN origin; it may be *Parry 11* built in 1895 and later owned by Hugh McKnight; or it may be *Fram,* which was cut up shortly after these pictures were taken.

Tractors are out in front, with the helm not yet fixed. The boat in the foreground may be *Ross,* which was used at the start of the 1950s and was fitted with a cabin by the late 1950s.

Ross at Park Head rally 2008.

ROSS

Built in 1847, for the Birmingham Canal Navigations Co. (the BCN), Ross is now the only one of the BCN fleet of iceboats in working condition, and is among the oldest working narrow boats on British canals.

Ross, which was horse drawn, cleared iced up sections of canal between the mines on Cannock Chase and the power stations in Walsall and Wolverhampton that they supplied with coal.

ROSS IS ON LOAN TO THE MUSEUM.

BLACK COUNTRY LIVING MUSEUM

Rocking the boat; James Williams is the short man on the right with his leg sticking out.

Friar Bridge – Pelsall Junction, the entrance to the Cannock Extension Canal from Pelsall Common. James Williams has his hand on the pole. Notice that they are using long-handled tongs to pull out blocks of ice to clear the narrows.

Leonard Leigh tugs also breaking a road on the Wyrley & Essington Canal to get the coal through.

The most dangerous part of the operation – rocking the boat to break up the ice.

This photo shows the technique of how the boat was drawn up on to the ice; the men then rocked the boat to break the ice underneath.

Above left: Pelsall Junction with the Cannock Extension Canal under the bridge, 2009.

Above right: Pelsall Common, looking toward the Junction, 2009.

One of the last coal boats from Cannock on the W&E; possibly Caggy Stevens, *c.* 1970. (JH)

Above and right:
The Tame Valley
Canal being
cleared of ice, early
twentieth century.
Barr Beacon can
be seen in the
distance in the
view from 2004.
This canal is rarely
boated these days.

Ice-breaking with
horses, early
twentieth century,
on the Tame Valley
Canal. (Pratt)

Wolverhampton

Wolverhampton started its existence as an Anglo Saxon settlement, later developing into a medieval market place. During the Middle Ages, Wolverhampton's wealth and status derived mainly from the wool trade, though as the seventeenth and eighteenth centuries came along, the focus shifted gradually – as in many other Midland towns – toward the metal trades. Each town came to specialise – but with some overlapping – into particular branches of metal goods; Wednesbury in pipes and gun barrels, Sedgley, Gornal and Coseley for nails, Walsall with its bridles, bits and harnesses, Bilston in enamelware, Birmingham in the 'Toy trade', while Wolverhampton and next-door Willenhall manufactured locks and buckles. The Chubb building still overlooks Top Lock today. Sketchley's directory of 1770, only two years before the canal arrives, lists 118 lockmakers, producing twenty-six different types of lock. There were 260 lock makers by 1841, and about sixty-five key makers. An expensive (very) pair of shoe buckles might fetch 10-15 guineas, such was the fashion of the day. Men who spent their lives filing lock mechanisms were often identified by the deformities of a displaced shoulder and crooked right knee.

In *A History of Wolverhampton*, the author, Chris Upton, writes that in the last quarter of the eighteenth century, three-quarters of the town's manufactured goods were for export; this inevitably placed a lot of pressure on the road system. Earlier in that same century, John Ward told a House of Commons Enquiry that the road to Birmingham was impassable during winter months due to the volume of coal and iron.

Toll roads (Turnpike Trusts) were part of the solution, and long-distance travel by coach relied on them heavily. In 1772, the Birmingham–Wolverhampton and the Staffordshire & Worcestershire Canal opened at just the right time to promote further growth, and several Wolverhampton businessmen put their money into the venture. As soon as the canal and its twenty locks were up and running, local merchants and manufacturers jostled for position along its banks. By 1851, the town boasted of having thirteen coal merchants, while passenger boats had been running a daily service to and from Birmingham for more than a decade.

Aldersley Junction

Aldersley Junction, right at the bottom of the Wolverhampton 21 Locks, was the first gateway for the BCN into a wider world. The planning for the early Birmingham Canal included a junction with the Staffordshire & Worcestershire Canal. This was to be a most important gateway down to the River Severn at Aldersley. It came with the Act of Parliament in 1768. The act stated that the junction should be at Autherley, otherwise Aldersley, and during the last few hundred years it has been called The Junction, Old Autherley Junction, Autherley Junction, Autherley 1 Junction, and finally Aldersley Junction. So just to confuse matters, when the Birmingham & Liverpool Junction Canal opened in 1835, someone wisely called that junction Autherley. So I hope that's now all clear.

Aldersley's position as an important gateway continued until the Birmingham & Fazeley Canal opened in 1789. Later on in 1815, the Worcester & Birmingham Canal opened, thus granting another way out from the BCN to the south. Obviously, as each exit in turn opened, it lessened the traffic at the early junction, but there was always a high volume going through Aldersley. As a consequence, both the Staffs & Worcs and the BCN built important company offices right at the connection of the two waterways.

Our black and white photos of Aldersley show the junction during the 1950s. The four-storey building known as Autherly House was built in 1773-74. Connected to it were two semi-detached buildings known as Oxley Moor buildings. Today, of course, as our later photograph shows, all the buildings have gone, but at least the lower parts of the structures have been tastefully left to offer a kind of porthole into the past. Right until the middle of the twentieth century, Aldersley was always a busy spot, with as many as 20,000 boats per year coming through the bottom lock of the Wolverhampton 21 alone.

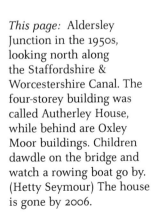

This page: Aldersley Junction in the 1950s, looking north along the Staffordshire & Worcestershire Canal. The four-storey building was called Autherley House, while behind are Oxley Moor buildings. Children dawdle on the bridge and watch a rowing boat go by. (Hetty Seymour) The house is gone by 2006.

83

An FMC and a BW boat prepare to enter the BCN at the bottom lock. (HS) Both the S&W and the BCN had offices at this location. A bridge now sits across the junction at the tail of the lock, 2006.

Wolverhampton top lock, early twentieth century, with boats waiting their turn to go into the lock. The Victoria basin off to the left was a busy wharfing area. Jane Doley was murdered along this arm just before the First World War (see *Canal Crimes*, R. H. Davies (Amberley, 2010)). In 1955, Thomas Clayton's boats *Frome* and *Jardine* are tied up by a bridge that has now been removed. The gas boats did frequent trips to collect by-products from the gasworks situated halfway down the locks. In 2008, the lock cottages are still pretty much the same, but the rest of the scene has changed, with colourful planting taking the place of the bridge into the old basin. The Victoria basin has been reduced to a short stub.

Climbing up the Wolverhampton 21, with the Cannock Road Bridge overhead.

Above and left:
Halfway down the Wolverhampton locks at lock 10 with Thomas Clayton boat *Umea.* Clayton's conducted a regular trade in creosote to a place on the S&W. Now, factories and tall chimneys have been razed to make way for a larger chimney of the municipal incinerator.

Leaving Wolverhampton behind, we are now on the main line at Coseley. Here, in 1975, we see one of the successful Midland Company's of the past –the Cannon Gas works. In the foreground are some of the boats belonging to Alfred Matty, who managed to make a living out of the canal into the 1970s. (KH) New housing has replaced Cannon, and the pub to the left has also gone. Public houses have been closing in the Midlands, sometimes at the rate of seven or eight a week. Coseley Tunnel is just in front and around the bend in the canal.

In the past, there were hundreds of coal yards throughout the BCN. Today, there is only one left on the canal banks, and here we see the Wilfruna Coal Company during the 1970s, but they were still active in coal distribution during 2010. (KH)

Old Canals and New Museums

This may appear a rather strange title to conclude the book, but I would like to finish off with a few pictures of canals that have vanished in the course of time, and a few images from the Black Country Living Museum. If the museum didn't exist, then much of what the Black Country stood for, its industries, its housing and its social life would only be found between the covers of books. Certainly the museum makes the most of the Dudley canal that runs through its grounds, and also Lord Ward's branch that was used for limestone processing. Each year, the museum adds a little more to its collection, maybe another house, perhaps a shop or bridge, but it also cares for several historic working boats and hosts working boat rallies. So far in the book, we have looked at changing places, the removal of old factories and back-to-back housing, which has often been replaced by high-tech units and modern apartments, but the first contrasting pictures here show changing boats. Yes, the steam-powered narrow boat *President*, possibly the most famous narrow boat of all time, has itself gone through a few makeovers. The boat did certainly start life with Fellows, Morton & Clayton as a steamer, but during the 1950s, she served as a maintenance boat for British Waterways with a diesel engine – a very different boat indeed. And it wasn't until recent times that she was reconverted to her original type.

In 1981, the BCN Society published a book by Richard Chester-Browne that highlighted the lost canals of Birmingham. It's a fascinating book to peruse, and in the introduction, Richard explains that it was during his years as a student, between 1974 an 1977, that he did a pretty thorough survey of the Birmingham canals: those that had survived the wilderness years of the 1950s and 60s and those that hadn't. He calculated that the BCN at the height of its operations had some 174 miles of canal, but by the time of his investigation, some 60 miles had been lost. They may have just succumbed to reed and plant overgrowth due to lack of use or maintenance, or they may very well have been purposely filled in and built upon. Of course, it is fascinating to take a map and try to discover the course of old canals to see what is left, but there is also a melancholy side to the venture – even if you don't personally remember them.

Certainly, I don't claim to be an expert on canals – but like many folks, I just love them. And I think that those of us who have come to appreciate and take solace in our man-made watery corridors, for whatever reasons, must do what we can to ensure that we don't lose any more.

Hence, dear canal aficionados, the last few photographs. But don't be downhearted, for as you read this book, local canal societies and other bodies are actively engaged in trying to bring back some of those lost lines. I will not name them all, but we may read in the canal press of the Lapal canal society, who would love to reinstate the Dudley No. 2 canal. This would link the Dudley canals again with the Birmingham & Worcester via Gosty and the Lapal tunnels. There is the Lichfield & Hatherton Canal Society, who are working to reinstate sections of the Wyrley & Essington Canal. This would provide a marvellous north-eastern gateway to the BCN, and a through route to the Staffs & Worcs. And then, of course, there are the smaller groups who have just gone along and cleaned up the bit of canal where they live – such as the section of the Ridgacre branch. So, let's be positive and see what the future holds, or maybe even better get involved yourself?

British Waterways boat *President* some time during the 1950s, showing the stables at the bottom of the Audlem flight on the Shropshire Union Canal. According to Richard Thomas, archivist of Friends of the *President*, the boat spent some time based on the Macclesfield Canal, perhaps in the Marple area. Just behind and only just visible is the Yarwoods-built tug *Beeston*, powered by a twin-cylinder Armstrong Siddeley engine. The *President* is now based at the Black Country Living Museum.

The entrance to the Black Country Living Museum, Tipton.

A useful mooring inside the BCLM. On the right is another FMC boat, *Peacock*, while in the distance is the wonderful cast-iron bridge that was taken from its location at Broad Street, Wolverhampton, right next to the Broad Street basin and top lock. Broad Street now has a nice new bridge, wide enough to take the modern traffic flows of the ring road. In the foreground is one of the few remaining horse-drawn fly boats, now operated by Sue Day of the Horse Boat Society.

Right: The old lime kilns became a feature in the BCLM. Lime manufacture was a big part of Lord Ward's operations, and the rough limestone was dug from under the Dudley hills, brought to the kilns and burnt into powder. The lime was then utilised for construction, or for reducing the acidity in agricultural land. (KH)

Below: Lime kilns and recent developments in the BCLM, 2009.

A Sunday School party in the early twentieth century takes a trip on the Tipton and Toll End Communication Canal near Toll End. From almost the same location today, looking towards Great Bridge, from the canal bridge, the housing has altered, and the Methodist church that used to sit at the end of Aston Street has also long gone.

Great Bridge and the Haines Branch in the 1960s. This branch came off the Walsall Canal just below Ryder's Green bottom lock. Here we see boats belonging to the Willow Wren fleet delivering timber to Cox's wood yard all the way from Brentford. The canal originally went some distance beyond Tame Road Bridge, which can be seen in the distance, to serve collieries and an ironworks. (DW) The track of the canal can still be seen, while buildings to the right show that they had a relationship with the canal at one time. Sheepwash Urban Park, a relatively new nature area, has taken the place of the collieries, clay pits and brick works of former days.

Gate repair at the top of the Bradley locks during the 1950s. I must admit, I don't remember this canal, but its path can easily be traced from the bridge near Willingsworth School. On the other side of the bridge, the canal can be followed to its connection with the Walsall Canal some few hundred yards distant. (WK)

The Bradley locks ran up this gentle slope toward the Bradley loop. 2010.